First World War
and Army of Occupation
War Diary
France, Belgium and Germany

58 DIVISION
Headquarters, Branches and Services
Royal Army Ordnance Corps
Deputy Assistant Director Ordnance Services
16 January 1917 - 31 May 1919

WO95/2994/4

The Naval & Military Press Ltd
www.nmarchive.com
Published in association with The National Archives

Published by

The Naval & Military Press Ltd

Unit 10 Ridgewood Industrial Park,

Uckfield, East Sussex,

TN22 5QE England

Tel: +44 (0) 1825 749494

www.naval-military-press.com

www.nmarchive.com

This diary has been reprinted in facsimile from the original. Any imperfections are inevitably reproduced and the quality may fall short of modern type and cartographic standards.

© Crown Copyright
Images reproduced by permission of The National Archives, London, England, 2015.

Contents

Document type	Place/Title	Date From	Date To
Heading	WO95/2994/4		
Heading	58th Division D.A. Dir. Ordnance Services Jan 1917-May 1919		
Miscellaneous	58th Division	03/11/1917	03/11/1917
War Diary	Calais	16/01/1917	16/01/1917
War Diary	Boulogne	18/01/1917	18/01/1917
War Diary	St Pol	19/01/1917	22/01/1917
War Diary	Frevent	23/01/1917	05/02/1917
War Diary	Lucheux	06/02/1917	20/02/1917
War Diary	Henu	25/02/1917	25/03/1917
War Diary	La Cauchie	26/02/1917	21/03/1917
War Diary	Lucheux	28/03/1917	30/04/1917
Heading	War Diary Of D.A.D.O.S. (58th Divn) From 4/5/17 To 27/5/17 Vol 5		
War Diary		04/05/1917	27/05/1917
War Diary	Achiet Le Grand	01/06/1917	31/07/1917
War Diary	In The Field	01/08/1917	29/08/1917
Heading	War Diary Of D.A.D.O.S. 58th Divn From 1st Sept 1917 To 30th Sept 1917		
War Diary	Poperinghe	01/09/1917	26/09/1917
War Diary	Zutkerke	28/09/1917	29/09/1917
Heading	War Diary Of D.A.D.O.S. 58th Divn From 1st Oct 1917 To 31st Oct 1917 Vol 10		
War Diary	Zutkerke	01/10/1917	21/10/1917
War Diary	Poperinghe	22/10/1917	29/10/1917
Heading	War Diary Of DADOS 58th (London) Divn For November 1917		
War Diary	Poperinghe	01/11/1917	26/11/1917
Heading	War Diary Of DADOS 58th (London) Division For December 1917		
War Diary	Nielles Les Blequin	05/12/1917	05/12/1917
War Diary	Elverdinghe	08/12/1917	28/12/1917
Heading	War Diary Of DADOS 58th (London) Divn For January 1918		
War Diary	Elverdinghe	02/01/1918	02/01/1918
War Diary	Proven	08/01/1918	17/01/1918
War Diary	Corbie	19/01/1918	31/01/1918
Heading	Diary Of DADOS 58th London Division For February 1918		
War Diary	Corbie	02/02/1918	02/02/1918
War Diary	Villequiers Aumont	08/02/1918	22/02/1918
War Diary	Ognes	24/02/1918	27/02/1918
Heading	War Diary Of D.A.D.O.S. 58th Divn For Month Of March 1918		
War Diary	Ognes	03/03/1918	21/03/1918
War Diary	Noyon	22/03/1918	23/03/1918
War Diary	Chiry	24/03/1918	24/03/1918
War Diary	Estrees	25/03/1918	27/03/1918
War Diary	Compiegne	29/03/1918	29/03/1918

Heading	War Diary Of D.A.D.O.S. 58th London Division For April 1918		
War Diary	Blerancourt	01/04/1918	01/04/1918
War Diary	Amiens	03/04/1918	03/04/1918
War Diary	Saleux	04/04/1918	30/04/1918
Heading	War Diary Of D.A.D.O.S. 58th Divn From 1st May To 31st May 1918		
War Diary	St Riquier	01/05/1918	02/05/1918
War Diary	Molliens Au Bois	07/05/1918	12/05/1918
War Diary	Beaucourt	16/05/1918	26/05/1918
Heading	War Diary Of DADOS 58th (London) Divn From 1st June 1918 To 30th June 1918		
War Diary	Ebarts Farm	01/06/1918	06/06/1918
War Diary	Cavillon	10/06/1918	18/06/1918
War Diary	Ebarts Farm	19/06/1918	28/06/1918
Heading	War Diary Of D.A.D.O.S. 58th Divn For July 1918		
War Diary	Beaucourt	01/07/1918	31/07/1918
War Diary	Ebarts Farm (Beaucourt)	01/08/1918	01/08/1918
War Diary	Querrieu	04/08/1918	10/08/1918
War Diary	St. Gratien	13/08/1918	13/08/1918
War Diary	Heilly	24/08/1918	29/08/1918
War Diary	Near Bray	30/08/1918	30/08/1918
Heading	War Diary Of DADOS 58th Div For September 1918		
War Diary	Near Bray	01/09/1918	05/09/1918
War Diary	Maricourt	07/09/1918	08/09/1918
War Diary	Moislains	10/09/1918	22/09/1918
War Diary	Montauban	23/09/1918	24/09/1918
War Diary	Mingoval	26/09/1918	27/09/1918
War Diary	Sains-En Gohelle	29/09/1918	29/09/1918
Heading	War Diary DADOS 58th (London) Division For October 1918		
War Diary	Sains En Gohelle	01/10/1918	03/10/1918
War Diary	Bully Grenay	07/10/1918	14/10/1918
War Diary	Fouquieres	16/10/1918	18/10/1918
War Diary	Bersee	19/10/1918	21/10/1918
War Diary	Planard	22/10/1918	02/11/1918
War Diary	Nomain	04/11/1918	08/11/1918
War Diary	Rumegies	09/11/1918	11/11/1918
War Diary	Basecles	12/11/1918	12/11/1918
War Diary	Beloeil	13/11/1918	20/11/1918
War Diary	Peruwelz	21/11/1918	28/11/1918
Heading	War Diary Of DADOS 58th Division For December 1918		
War Diary	Peruwelz	02/12/1918	27/12/1918
Heading	War Diary Of DADOS 58th Division For January 1919		
War Diary	Peruwelz	01/01/1919	29/01/1919
Heading	War Diary Of DADOS 58th (London Divin) For February 1919		
War Diary	Peruwelz	05/02/1919	28/02/1919
Heading	War Diary Of DADOS 58th Div For March 1919		
War Diary	Peruwelz	03/03/1919	17/03/1919
War Diary	Tournai	19/03/1919	31/03/1919
Heading	War Diary Of D.A.D.O.S. 58th Divn For April 1919		
War Diary	Tournai	08/04/1919	29/04/1919
Heading	War Diary Of D.A.D.O.S. 58th Divn For May 1919		
War Diary	Tournai	01/05/1919	31/05/1919

WO 95/2994/4

58TH DIVISION

D.A.DIR. ORDNANCE SERVICES
JAN 1917 - MAY 1919

AQ
58th Divn

Attached War Diary
for Sept 1917, which
should have been
forwarded last month,
was overlooked.
The omission is
regretted
    [Signature] Capt
       DADOS
       58th Divn

3/10/17

Army Form C. 2118.

WAR DIARY
or
INTELLIGENCE SUMMARY.
(Erase heading not required.)

Army Telegram DADOS 3872 Vol 1. 2

Place	Date	Hour	Summary of Events and Information	Remarks and references to Appendices
Calais	16/7		Arrived with advanced party of DHQ – left for Boulogne – arrived same day	
Boulogne	18/7		Left for St Pol	
St Pol	19/7		Called on DDOS IIIrd Army	
"	22/7		Left for Arras	
Arras	23/7		Borrowed Sergt Jordan & loan of horses of 23rd Div (from no DHDS mule 3 in no) & driver to Sand	
"	29/7		HQ 58th Division arrived at station. Le Grand	
Bréau le Sec	28/7		Moved from Arras to Bréau le Grand	
"	30/7		S Co. Reg. & Amm S/Sergt Long went for instruction 35th Divn at Roclincourt	
"	2/7		S Co. Reg. & Amm S/Sergt Hall left	
"	3/7		Went to IIIrd Army re Box respirators	
"	5/7		Sent lorries to Ruitz	
Ruitz	6/7		DHQ moved to Ruitz	
"	8/7		Visited ADOS XVIII Corps & I.O.M. with debit regd for A.H.Q.	

WAR DIARY
or
INTELLIGENCE SUMMARY.
(Erase heading not required.)

Army Form C. 2118.

Instructions regarding War Diaries and Intelligence Summaries are contained in F. S. Regs., Part II. and the Staff Manual respectively. Title pages will be prepared in manuscript.

Place	Date	Hour	Summary of Events and Information	Remarks and references to Appendices
Ruckem	10/7/17		D.D.O.S. III"d Army visited Office. Bought Machine for Soles.	
"	12/7/17		La Cauchie for Sub Sigs. 12 attached men reported. Box repairers issued.	
"	13/4/17		Hodin Div Workshops. Ammunion Solvers Storeware.	
"	14/7/17		Invest re clearing railheads to	
"	15/7/17		Curete trench issued	
"	16/7/17		A.D.O.S. XVIII Corps - visited H.Q.C.a.	
"	20/7/17		D. H.Q. moved to Hénu	
Hénu	25/7/17		Office moved to Hénu	
La Cauchie	26/7/17		" " La Cauchie	
"	28/7/17		D.H.Q. moved to Bavincourt	
"	2/8/17		Cleared Ruckem. A.D.O.S. XVIII Corps Called	
"	7/8/17		Went to St. Pol. with Dist. Gas Officer to see Capt. Hadley Army Gas Officer re Gas appearances to who confirmed D.R.O. - Ammunion stop drilled	
"	8/8/17		Boots (3345) received from Base.	
"	13/8/17		D.D.O.S. at D.H.Q. - G.O.C. inspected dump & shops.	

Army Form C. 2118.

WAR DIARY
or
INTELLIGENCE SUMMARY.
(Erase heading not required.)

Instructions regarding War Diaries and Intelligence Summaries are contained in F. S. Regs., Part II. and the Staff Manual respectively. Title pages will be prepared in manuscript.

Place	Date	Hour	Summary of Events and Information	Remarks and references to Appendices
La Cauchy	1917 20th		Transferred to VII Corps.	
"	3/7		Called on A.D.O.S. VII Corps	
"	21/7		A.D.O.S. went through books re promised to send pro formas - moved 48th A.F.A. Bgde to 14th Divn. 750 A.F.A. Bgde to 30th Divn.	
Ruchteux	28/7		Moves from La Caucie to Ruchteux	
"	30/7		Moved 197 M.C. Co. to 9th Divn 615th "	
			44 " 575th "	
			206 { from England third.	
			214	
			215	

A B Jarrett Col.

D.A.D.O.S. 58th LONDON DIVISION.

WAR DIARY
or
INTELLIGENCE SUMMARY

Army Form C. 2118.

DA 575 38

Place	Date	Hour	Summary of Events and Information	Remarks and references to Appendices
	1/4/17		Moved from Auchew to Frohen le Grand	
	2.	—	Called on ADVS XIX Corps	
	3.	—	Moved HQ to 58 Dv RA 290 Bde 291 Bde DAC V X Y Z in Batteries all to 21 Div	
	3.	—	ADVS XIX Corps called	
	5.	—	Move from Frohen le Grand to Bus les Artois. Called on ADVS X Corps	
	6.	—	Drew ciup[?] for staring tents asked for arie 982235	
	6.	—	sent to Bouquemaison with O.C. Battl. to see Capt. Nielsen re hospitn. of Division in refd of Corps taking over our equipment	
	9.	—	Visited HQ 173 Bde RA at La Cauchie, closed Sailly Poubieux[?]	
	10.		22 Trucks consigned in error by MFO	
	10.		Visited ADVS Achiet le Grand re moving through this[?] there	
	12.		to Doullens & Hesrieu[?] to arrange for Trucks to move to Achiet	
		6.30 pm	move cancelled	
	16		Started moving to Achiet le Grand	

WAR DIARY
or
INTELLIGENCE SUMMARY.
(Erase heading not required.)

Army Form C. 2118.

Place	Date	Hour	Summary of Events and Information	Remarks and references to Appendices
	20.4.17		Moved office to better site french trenches adj. V Corps	
	21-		visited 173 Brigade. A "Eagle" AOD arrived for instruction	
	23		A. Eagle appointed to 25 Div as DADOS Lt Turton arr arrived for instruction	
	24-		Cept Forrest proceeded to Calais from leave to Boulogne on leave	
	25		Collected & shaft erection for iron weep Bar, 30-pitch on arrival we found the is an insufficient condition.	
	26-		Issued me clothing under B/M 5290 B/G dut car & Bn Supply column. 1k slops for repairs signed Say 2/Lt. Gaw a/c 273. Complete statement of stores taken raken thorises to Swaville	
	27-		Sent 3 motorcycle clutch centres Base	
	28		Regarded a firm case of Manber have been sent by C29/118a to HQ.	
	29-		Collected 25 sets of Pack saddlery from DO SC. 12 from Bus 42 from Hadley trailer despatches 800 3 67 901 reverse Instructor Bryar to draw the SB from 50.56 to places	
	30		1st Ferrier for H Keucker ranen, wheels required	M.Tuckwell 42*y SSOUs

CONFIDENTIAL
****

W A R   D I A R Y

OF

D.A.O.S (58th Divn)

From 1/5/17
To 27/5/17

Army Form C. 2118.

WAR DIARY
or
INTELLIGENCE SUMMARY.
(Erase heading not required.)

Instructions regarding War Diaries and Intelligence Summaries are contained in F.S. Regs., Part II. and the Staff Manual respectively. Title pages will be prepared in manuscript.

Place	Date	Hour	Summary of Events and Information	Remarks and references to Appendices
	4/1/7		2nd consignment winter clothing dispatched to Base.	
	5/1/7		I returned from leave	
	10/5/7		Lieut Irwin went to 63rd Divn on orders received from Corps Sigs	
	12/5/7		Sig Cor Sarg + Corpl Brizenden went to Red Cross Hospice S'Omer	
	27/5/7		Corpl Ruty + Corpl Brizenden returned	

A.S Seward Lt
D.S.O.S 1st Divn.
1/5/17.

WAR DIARY
INTELLIGENCE SUMMARY
(Erase heading not required.)

Army Form C.2118.

DADS 5-6

June 1916 J.H.6

Place	Date	Hour	Summary of Events and Information	Remarks and references to Appendices
Achiet grand	1/6	2/6 9ᵃ	London Regt cont in two Captured Machine Guns	
"	6/6	9ᵃ	2nd S/Sgt Hall proceeded to England on leave	
"	"	10ᵃ	Rfn Richards Rfn Reynolds Rfn Hill went to III Army Rest Camp	
"	"	11ᵃ	Sergt Hendebrick proceeded on leave to England	
"	"	"	S/Cpl Bordsley proceeded to England on leave	
"	"	30ᵐ	100 Yukon packs received	
"	"		Cancelled all indents for Antiga Syphon G. HQ 03/15/225	

A.D. Jennerley
DADS 58th Div.

WAR DIARY
INTELLIGENCE SUMMARY

Army Form C. 2118.

DADOS 7578
July 1917
Vol 7

Place	Date	Hour	Summary of Events and Information	Remarks and references to Appendices
Achiet le Grand	6/7		Transferred from Vth Corps to IV Corps.	
			Called on ADOS VI Corps.	
	7/7		Transferred from IV to III Corps	
			Went to Rocquigny to make arrangements re taking over from 42nd Divⁿ	
	9/7		Moved from Achiet le Grand to Rocquigny	
	10/7		Moved from Rocquigny to Bus	
	23/7		Went to Warlus to arrange taking over from VIth Divⁿ	
	28/7		Moved from Bus to Warlus	
	31/7		Called on ADOS XVII Corps. Transferred to XVII Corps.	

A.B. Drummond Col
DADOS 3rd Brn

Army Form C. 2118.

WAR DIARY
or
INTELLIGENCE SUMMARY.
(Erase heading not required.)

DADES 58 Vol 8

Instructions regarding War Diaries and Intelligence Summaries are contained in F. S. Regs., Part II. and the Staff Manual respectively. Title pages will be prepared in manuscript.

Place	Date	Hour	Summary of Events and Information	Remarks and references to Appendices
In the Field	1/6		A.D.O.S. XIII Corps Called	
	2/6/17		Called on 2/5th & 2/6th & 510 C.A.S.C.	
	3/6		Brigade Conference at H.Q. 174th Brigade	
	19/6/17		A.D.O.S. called	
	20/6/17		Changes from Lowkow to Northern Base	
	24/6/17		Started move from Wardara to Poperinghe	
	28/6/17		Moves from Poperinghe to A.30 Central	
			23rd D.A. from 46th to 58th Div	
	29/6/17		" from A.30 Central to A.27 D.S.O.	

A.D. Kennard Col
D.D.O.S. 5th Dir
6/7/17

WAR DIARY
or
INTELLIGENCE SUMMARY.
(Erase heading not required.)

Army Form C. 2118.

Vol 9

War Diary of DADOS 58th Divn
from 1st Oct 1917 to 30 Nov 1917

Fleming Col
DADOS
58th Divn

Army Form C. 2118.

WAR DIARY
or
INTELLIGENCE SUMMARY.
(Erase heading not required.)

Instructions regarding War Diaries and Intelligence Summaries are contained in F. S. Regs., Part II. and the Staff Manual respectively. Title pages will be prepared in manuscript.

Place	Date	Hour	Summary of Events and Information	Remarks and references to Appendices
POPERINGHE	1/9/17		23rd D.A. marched to 47th Divn.	
"	3/9/17		58th D.A. moved to 58th Divn.	
"	10/9/17		23rd D.A. from 58th to 28th Divn.	
"	14/9/17		Capt. A.D.Tennant proceeded on leave.	
"	16/9/17		48th D.A. marched to 58th Divn.	
"	17/9/17		ADOS XVIII Corps called.	
"	26/9/17		Capt. A.D.Tennant reports to 8.7th Divn. To take over duties of DADOS	
			Capt. K.C. GRZIG reports to 58th Divn. do.	
			Divn. moved to ZUTKERKE. Packed MATTEN. 58th DA DQ moved to	
ZUTKERKE	28/9/17		to 48th Divn. ADOS XIX Corps called.	
"	29/9/17		Arriews farewell & Staff Capt. 1745170 Reon.	

1/10/17.

Murphy Capt
DADOS
58th Division

Army Form C. 2118.

WAR DIARY
or
INTELLIGENCE SUMMARY.
(Erase heading not required.)

Vol 10

War Diary of D.A.D.P.S 68th Divn
from 1 Oct 1917 to 31 Dec 1917

Nothing doing.
D.A.D.P.S
remarks

Army Form C. 2118.

WAR DIARY
or
INTELLIGENCE SUMMARY.
(Erase heading not required.)

Instructions regarding War Diaries and Intelligence Summaries are contained in F. S. Regs., Part II. and the Staff Manual respectively. Title pages will be prepared in manuscript.

Place	Date	Hour	Summary of Events and Information	Remarks and references to Appendices
ZUTKERKE	1/10/17 to 6/10/17		Awaiting Brigades & Units of Divn. to Rendezvous	
"	7/10/17		Units Arrive in Divnal Area & ADOS XVIII Corps	
"	8/10/17		Units Arrive Area	
"	9/10/17 to 11/10/17		Arrival of Units, Units Clothing were Examined	
"	13/10/17		Arrival ADOS XIX Corps	
"	14/10/17		Arrival ADOS XIX Corps	
"	17/10/17 to 21/10/17		Awaiting Units	
POPERINGHE	22/10/17		Divn. moved to POPERINGHE (Rendezvous) PROVEN	
"	23/10/17		Arrival ADOS XVIII Corps 58th DA Reformed	
"	25/10/17		Rendevoud & Capt 58th DA	
"	27/10/17		Move to Divnal Dumps, 32nd DA from 32nd Div to 58th Div	
"	29/10/17		Arrival ADOS XVIII Corps	

31/10/17
H. Tunney (?) Col.
DADOS
58 Div Divn.

Army Form C. 2118.

WAR DIARY
or
INTELLIGENCE SUMMARY.
(Erase heading not required.)

War Diary of DADMS 53rd (Welsh) Divn
for November 1917

Kethring Col
DADMS
53rd Divn

4/1/11

Army Form C. 2118.

WAR DIARY
or
INTELLIGENCE SUMMARY.
(Erase heading not required.)

Instructions regarding War Diaries and Intelligence Summaries are contained in F. S. Regs., Part II. and the Staff Manual respectively. Title pages will be prepared in manuscript.

Place	Date	Hour	Summary of Events and Information	Remarks and references to Appendices
POPERINGHE	1/4/17		50th D.A. moved to TRUQUES AREA	
"	2/4/17		A.D.S. I Corps ammo Dump O.R.C. detachment sent to 50th D.S.	
"	3/4/17		Moved 50th D.S. to Blaio Road	
"	4/4/17		50th D.S. moved to ETAPLES area	
"	15/4/17		Moved HDQRS II Corps.	
"	17/4/17		Moved to PROVEN. Reached PROVEN.	
"	18/4/17		Moved 50th D.S.	
"	26/4/17		Moved to NIELLES-LES-BLEQUIN. Reached LUMBRES 8.30. Due 2.17 march for advance guard	[illegible signature]

War Diary 58 Bn (London) Division
for December 1917

Army Form C. 2118.

WAR DIARY
or
INTELLIGENCE SUMMARY.
(Erase heading not required.)

Instructions regarding War Diaries and Intelligence Summaries are contained in F. S. Regs., Part II. and the Staff Manual respectively. Title pages will be prepared in manuscript.

Place	Date	Hour	Summary of Events and Information	Remarks and references to Appendices
NIEPPES LES BLEQUIN	1/1/17	—	58th Div Arty moved to II Corps forward area (33rd Div Arty relieved 33rd Div)	
ELVERDINGHE	8/7/17		Divn moved to forward area. Ordnance Dumps established at ELVERDINGHE, Reserves ELVERDINGHE. 58th Div Arty started for Arras	
"	11/7/17		Capt R.C. GREIG proceeded on 14 days leave Paris to Eng Fwd.	
"	13/7/17		58th Div Arty moved from 76 to 50th Divn	
"	14/7/17 to 31/7/17		Ordnance Returns in by Corps Reg A.O.C.	
"	20/7/17 21/7/17 23/7/17 (24/7/17) 25/7/17 28/7/17		Corps dry rations ORcS II Corps DADOS 35 and 32nd Divn. ORcS II Corps	

R. Stirling (Capt) DADOS 58th Div (London) Divn

T2134. Wt. W708—776. 500000. 4/15. Sir J. C. & S.

DADOS 578 Army Form C. 2118.

3 FEB 1918

Ja/3

WAR DIARY
or
INTELLIGENCE SUMMARY.
(Erase heading not required.)

Instructions regarding War Diaries and Intelligence Summaries are contained in F. S. Regs., Part II. and the Staff Manual respectively. Title pages will be prepared in manuscript.

Place	Date	Hour	Summary of Events and Information	Remarks and references to Appendices
			War Diary of DADOS 60th (London) Divn for January 1918	
			R Long Col¹ DADOS 60th Divn	

T2134. Wt. W708—776. 500000. 4/15. Sir J. C. & S.

Army Form C. 2118.

WAR DIARY
or
INTELLIGENCE SUMMARY.
(Erase heading not required.)

Instructions regarding War Diaries and Intelligence Summaries are contained in F. S. Regs., Part II. and the Staff Manual respectively. Title pages will be prepared in manuscript.

Place	Date	Hour	Summary of Events and Information	Remarks and references to Appendices
EVERDINGHE	2/1/18	—	Capt K.C. GREIG D.A.D.O.S return from leave	
PROVEN	8/1/18		Division moved to PROVEN area. Rackhead PESELHOEK.	
"	11/1/18		Charles ADOS II Corps	
"	17/1/18		Charles DDOS Fifth Army.	
CORBIE	19/1/18		Moved to CORBIE Rackhead MATCH CAVE	
"	27/1/18		Charles ADOS VII Corps.	
"	31/1/18		Charles forward area & Div artillery DADOS.	

1/2/18

H Greig Capt
D.A.D.O.S
58th Div

Army Form C. 2118.

WAR DIARY
or
INTELLIGENCE SUMMARY.
(Erase heading not required.)

Diary of D.A.D.O.S. 58th London Division
for February 1918.

Kipling Capt
D.A.D.O.S.
58th Divn

Army Form C. 2118.

WAR DIARY
or
INTELLIGENCE SUMMARY.
(Erase heading not required.)

Place	Date	Hour	Summary of Events and Information	Remarks and references to Appendices
CONDE 2/9/18	2/9/18	—	Trains DDOS SyM Army	
VILLERS AUMONT	8/9/18		Division + DADOS moves to VILLEQUIERS AUMONT. Railhead HAM	
"	17/9/18		Railhead changes to ATTILLY.	
"	15/9/18		Capt R.C. GRIEVE, D.A.D.O.S. proceeds to RouEN. Entrance Exam in course of Instruction	
"	18/9/18 24/9/18		3 Canv. Bag. overhaul DDOS III Corps	
"	24/9/18		Office + Dump moves to OGNIES	
OGNIES	27/9/18		Div H.Q. moves to QUIETCY	

3/10/18

R. Strong Colonel
DADOS
3rd Army

WAR DIARY
or
INTELLIGENCE SUMMARY.

(Erase heading not required.)

Army Form C. 2118.

DADOS 58 D

Place	Date	Hour	Summary of Events and Information	Remarks and references to Appendices
			War Diary of DADOS 58th Divn for month of March 1918	
			Keeling (Capt) AOD DADOS 58th London Divn	

Army Form C. 2118.

WAR DIARY
or
INTELLIGENCE SUMMARY.
(Erase heading not required.)

Instructions regarding War Diaries and Intelligence Summaries are contained in F. S. Regs., Part II. and the Staff Manual respectively. Title pages will be prepared in manuscript.

Place	Date	Hour	Summary of Events and Information	Remarks and references to Appendices
OIGNIES	1/3/18		Capt. McGREW DADOS returns from Commission Course. Posted APTINX	
do	4/3/18 to 21/3/18		Departmental Routine	
NOYON	22/3/18		Move to NOYON owing to situation	
	23/3/18		Evacuation of Horses. Dumped at APTINX destroyed. Large numbers to corner & equipment fell into enemy hands on 24/3/18	
CHIRY	24/3/18		Move Div H.Q. to CHIRY. Div HQ is CAMELIN. Lines from R.A.S. suspended	
ESTREES	28/3/18		Moved to ESTREES ST DENNIS owing to enemy advance	
	27/3/18		Group H.Q. of Obs. advancing on CHIRY. belongs to 2000 aeroplane of enemy	
COMPIEGNE	29/3/18		Moved H.Q. to COMPIEGNE. Posted COMPIEGNE	

Craig (Capt)
D.A.D.O.S
58th (London) Division

Army Form C. 2118.

WAR DIARY
or
INTELLIGENCE SUMMARY.
(Erase heading not required.)

War Diary of R.E. of
58th London Division
for April 1918

Return to C in C'
R.E. of
58th Division

1628

Army Form C. 2118.

WAR DIARY
or
INTELLIGENCE SUMMARY.
(Erase heading not required.)

Instructions regarding War Diaries and Intelligence Summaries are contained in F. S. Regs., Part II. and the Staff Manual respectively. Title pages will be prepared in manuscript.

Place	Date	Hour	Summary of Events and Information	Remarks and references to Appendices
BIERANCOURT	1/4/18		DADO at BIERANCOURT. Burgo & Railhead COMPIEGNE	
AMIENS	2/4/18		DADO moves to SALEUX.	
SALEUX	4/4/18		Offices & Dump established at SALEUX	
	5/4/18		Visits ADOS III Corps & Railhead (AMIENS)	
	13/4/18		Lunas D.GRANT CRAWFORD ADO opening for instructions	
	16/4/18		to advance on Amiens Rd. (Visits all DADOS 2nd Army office)	
	26/4/18		Visits ST RIQUIER for Billets	
	28/4/18		Moves to ST RIQUIER	
	30/4/18		Railhead changes to ST RIQUIER	
		1/5/18 P.		

H Greig Capt
D.A.D.O.S
58 (London) Division

Army Form C. 2118.

WAR DIARY
or
INTELLIGENCE SUMMARY.
(Erase heading not required.)

War Diary of DADOS 58th Division
from 1st July to 31st August 1918.

Nothing of interest to report.

Place	Date	Hour	Summary of Events and Information	Remarks and references to Appendices

Army Form C. 2118.

WAR DIARY
or
INTELLIGENCE SUMMARY.
(Erase heading not required.)

Instructions regarding War Diaries and Intelligence Summaries are contained in F. S. Regs., Part II. and the Staff Manual respectively. Title pages will be prepared in manuscript.

Place	Date	Hour	Summary of Events and Information	Remarks and references to Appendices
ST RIQUIER	1/5/18	—	Division in rest area. Reached ST RIQUIER	
"	2/5/18		Lieut F Frank Crawford ADS proceeded to Entrance Officer II Corps Troops for temporary duty.	
MOLLIENS	7/5/18		Division moved to MOLLIENS AU BOIS. Raised PICQUIGNY	
AU BOIS	9/5/18		Cases in A.D.S. III Corps.	
"	10/5/18		D.D.G.S. IV ARMY paid visit.	
"	13/5/18		Lieut F Frank Crawford reported for duty from temporary duty.	
BEAUCOURT	14/5/18		Remained ADS moved to CONTAY. Divn moved to EBARTS FARM (BEAUCOURT)	
"	20/5/18		Visited ADS III Corps.	
"	23/5/18		Lieut D Stuart Crawford ADS proceeded as to 4st Divisor for duty	
"	31/5/18		ADS III Corps reorganised	

A.Frank Crawford
D.A.D.O.S
Brig Genl

Army Form C. 2118.

WAR DIARY
or
INTELLIGENCE SUMMARY.

(Erase heading not required.)

Instructions regarding War Diaries and Intelligence Summaries are contained in F. S. Regs., Part II. and the Staff Manual respectively. Title pages will be prepared in manuscript.

Place	Date	Hour	Summary of Events and Information	Remarks and references to Appendices

War Diary of D.A.D.E.S. 58th (London) Division

From 1st June 1918 to 30th June 1918

R. Kemp Capt
R.A.M.C.
58th Div.

Army Form C. 2118.

WAR DIARY
or
INTELLIGENCE SUMMARY.
(Erase heading not required.)

Instructions regarding War Diaries and Intelligence Summaries are contained in F.S. Regs., Part II. and the Staff Manual respectively. Title pages will be prepared in manuscript.

Place	Date	Hour	Summary of Events and Information	Remarks and references to Appendices
EBARTS FARM	1/6/18		DHQ at CONTAY, Reserves MERICOURT.	
"	5/6/18		Last Consignment Units leaving Corps to BASE	
"	6/6/18		DHQ moved to MEZIERES AU BOIS	
CAVILLON	10/6/18		Used A Dumps moved to DHQ to CAVILLON	
"	11/6/18		ADOS 22nd Corps over DS Dumps	
"	12/6/18		do	
"	17/6/18		do	Corps empties for Dump ABBEVILLE
"	18/6/18		RDOS + Army Supply Depot	
EBARTS FARM	19/6/18		Office & Dump moved to EBARTS FARM. Nearest VEM+COURT	
"	20/6/18		Empties sent to stores F. Known Dumps	
"	23/6/18		Indeed changed to BRIANVILLE. Capt K.G. REIG DADOS proceeds to England on 14 days leave	
"	29/6/18		ADOS 3rd Corps invited Dumps	

W Bingley Capt
D.A.D.O.S. 58 LONDON DIVISION.

30/6/18

Army Form C. 2118.

WAR DIARY
or
INTELLIGENCE SUMMARY.
(Erase heading not required.)

Vol 19

War Diary of "D" Co 1/5 52nd Divn
1st Feb - 31st July 1918

W. Knight Major
1/D.A.C. 2/5
52nd Divn

11/9/?

Army Form C. 2118.

WAR DIARY
or
INTELLIGENCE SUMMARY.
(Erase heading not required.)

Instructions regarding War Diaries and Intelligence Summaries are contained in F. S. Regs., Part II. and the Staff Manual respectively. Title pages will be prepared in manuscript.

Place	Date	Hour	Summary of Events and Information	Remarks and references to Appendices
JEANCOURT	1/7/18		Divnl Office at EBARTS FARM. D.H.Q. BEAUVOIS RT. Reserve Ø BRUNIVILLE	
"	3/7/18		Major K.C. REID returned from leave.	
"	9am to 5.9.7/18		Departmental Routine. Sir Haigs.	
	1/8/18			

Helmers Major
D.A.D.O.S.
58th Divn

T2134. Wt. W708—776. 500000. 4/15. Sir J. C. & S.

Army Form C. 2118

Copy D.A.D.T. G.S. Jul 20

WAR DIARY
or
INTELLIGENCE SUMMARY.
(Erase heading not required.)

Instructions regarding War Diaries and Intelligence Summaries are contained in F.S. Regs., Part II. and the Staff Manual respectively. Title pages will be prepared in manuscript.

Place	Date	Hour	Summary of Events and Information	Remarks and references to Appendices
EBARTS FARM (BEAUCOURT) QUERRIEU	1/8/18		Div. in BEAUCOURT AREA. Railhead VIGNACOURT.	
	4/8/18		D.H.Q. moved to QUERRIEU. Supp & office moved to position near QUERRIEU	
	10/8/18		Railhead moved to POULAINVILLE.	
ST GRATIEN	13/8/18		A.H.Q. moved to ST GRATIEN. Supp & office moved to same place.	
HEILLY	24/8/18		Moved to HEILLY. D.H.Q. moved to same place.	
	28/8/18		Railhead moved to MERICOURT L'ABBAYE	
	29/8/18		EDGE HILL	
NEAR BRAY	30/8/18		Moved to position at 52 D.A.Y.C. near rear Div. H.Q.	

(Sd) K.G. Irish Gen.
D.A.D.T. 5th Division

T2134. Wt. W708-776. 500000. 4/15. Sir J.C. & S.

WAR DIARY
or
INTELLIGENCE SUMMARY.

Army Form C. 2118.

War Diary of DADOS 55th Div
for November 1918

Hastings Major
DADOS
55 Div
M.E.F.

8/12/18

Army Form C. 2118.

WAR DIARY
or
INTELLIGENCE SUMMARY.
(Erase heading not required.)

Place	Date	Hour	Summary of Events and Information	Remarks and references to Appendices
near BRAY	1/9/18		Location 62 D. L7 c. Railhead EDGEHILL.	
"	5/9/18		Railhead changed to CARNOY.	
MARICOURT	7/9/18		Office & Dump moves to MARICOURT.	
"	8/9/18		18th Div A.T.G moved from 12th Div to 58th Div.	
MOISLAINS	10/9/18		Moved to MOISLAINS. DHQ CURLU WOOD	
"	12/9/18		2/2 & 2/4 Bns London Regt amalgamated	
"	13/9/18		2/10th Bn London Regt arrived from 66th Div	
"	18/9/18		Infant. passes to rear for 1000 yds run (1st Class)	
"	22/9/18		Troops from Bavai & Rouen stopped.	
MONTAUBAN	23/9/18		Moved to MONTAUBAN. Railhead PLATEAU.	
"	24/9/18		25 & 58 Div Artilleries moved to DHQOS Askelon Bn.	
MINGOVAL	26/9/18		Div moved to VIII Corps 1st Army. DHR, TILLERS CHATEL Railhead FRÉVIN CAPELLE	
"			Base changed to Calais (Calonne A)	
"	27/9/18		Train forward to 701 Blanchet	
SAINS-EN GOHELLE	29/9/18		Moved to SAINS EN GOHELLE. Railhead BARLIN. 12th Div A.T.G moved from 21 Div to 58 Div	

A5834. Wt. W4973/M637 750,000 8/16 D. D. & L. Ltd. Forms/C.2118/13.

Army Form C. 2118.

WAR DIARY
or
INTELLIGENCE SUMMARY.
(Erase heading not required.)

Vol 22

War Diary of
D.A.D.O.S. 50th (London) Division
for
October 1918.

Rt Lieut Major
D.A.D.O.S
58th Div.

Place	Date	Hour	Summary of Events and Information	Remarks and references to Appendices

Army Form C. 2118.

WAR DIARY or INTELLIGENCE SUMMARY.

(Erase heading not required.)

Instructions regarding War Diaries and Intelligence Summaries are contained in F.S. Regs., Part II. and the Staff Manual respectively. Title pages will be prepared in manuscript.

Place	Date	Hour	Summary of Events and Information	Remarks and references to Appendices
SAINS EN GOHELLE	1/10/18	—	Dumps & Office moved from MINGOVAL to SAINS EN GOHELLE (Pankhead) BATTN	
	2/10/18		Divl Blanket received. 2nd D.A. moved to 58th Div	
BULLY GRENAY	3/10/18		Dumps & Office moved to BULLY GRENAY	
"	12/10/18		Div transferred from 8th to 1st Corps Fifth Army	
"	13/10/18		Moved 7th to DA to 24th Divn	
"	14/10/18		58th DA moved from 18th Corps Troops to 58th Divn	
FOUQUIERES	16/10/18		Dumps & Office moved to FOUQUIERES	
"	18/10/18		Four Ruora Arnold Clothing lorries posted at BULLY GRENAY. Capt W. KIRTON reported from 11th Corps for duty.	
BERSÉE	19/10/18		Office moved to BERSÉE. Dumps remaining at FOUQUIERES with long strings at BERSÉE	
"	21/10/18		Owing to shortage of transport & non-distribution of stores through operations, lorries from 2nd RAFA Reserve Park stopped except Rock Hironcles lorries to 1st Regt founded stores, 3rd RAFA Reserve moved from 1st Corps Troops to 58th Divn (move confirmed by ADOS 1st Corps)	
PLANARD	22/10/18		Office moved to PLANARD	
"	23/10/18		Packhead opened at CUINCHY	
"	24/10/18		Dumps moved to BERSÉE	

Army Form C. 2118.

WAR DIARY
or
INTELLIGENCE SUMMARY.
(Erase heading not required.)

Instructions regarding War Diaries and Intelligence Summaries are contained in F. S. Regs., Part II. and the Staff Manual respectively. Title pages will be prepared in manuscript.

Place	Date	Hour	Summary of Events and Information	Remarks and references to Appendices
PLANARD	25/10		Daily dump opened at PLANARD for all arms except Artillery. Capt HAMILTON proceeded to HAMRE	
	26/10		HAMRE Railhead moved to MARQUILLIES.	
	27/10		Capt PATRICK AOD reports for temporary duty	
			Part of reserve clothing brought from BULLY GRENAY & some Ordnance Dumps	
			for Divn. clothing opened at NOMAIN.	
	29/10		Divn Dump moved to NOMAIN	
	30/10		Railhead moves to DON. Bros moved to demie train	
	31/10		Remainder of reserve clothing received by light Railway from BULLY GRENAY.	

31/10/18

H. Smith Major
DADOS
38th Divn

WAR DIARY or INTELLIGENCE SUMMARY

Army Form C. 2118.

58 DAC
Nov 23

Place	Date	Hour	Summary of Events and Information	Remarks and references to Appendices
PLANARD	2-11-18	–	Office moved from PLANARD to NOMAIN	
NOMAIN	4-11-18		MAJOR K.C. GREIG moved to Divn Rail Station BERSÉE	
"	5-11-18		A.D.O.S. visited Dump	
"	7-11-18		MAJOR K.C. GREIG evacuated to C.C.S. DON.	
"	8-11-18		Railhead moved from DON to FRETIN.	
ROMEGIES	9-11-18		Office + Dump moved to ROMEGIES. Supplied issues from Base.	
"	10-11-18		Issue issues with clothing completed.	
"	11-11-19		ARMISTICE. A.D.O.S. 1st Corps created Dump. Office + Dump moved from ROMEGIES	
"			to BASECLES.	
BASECLES	12-11-18		Office + Dump moved from BASECLES to BELOEIL	
BELOEIL	13-11-18		Accepted issues from Base.	
"	15-11-18		242 A.F.A. Brigade transferred to Corps Troops.	
"	16-11-18		Visited A.D.O.S. 1st Corps. Four Corps lorries loaned	
"	17-11-18		Two Corps lorries broken down	
"	18-11-18		Issued unified Blanket demanded. 242 A.F.A. Brigade notified was	
"			transferred to 3rd Corps Troops + 1st 1st Corps Troops.	
"	20-11-18		Authority given to retain two Corps lorries until 24 F	

Army Form C. 2118.

WAR DIARY
or
INTELLIGENCE SUMMARY.
(Erase heading not required.)

Instructions regarding War Diaries and Intelligence
Summaries are contained in F. S. Regs., Part II.
and the Staff Manual respectively. Title pages
will be prepared in manuscript.

Place	Date	Hour	Summary of Events and Information	Remarks and references to Appendices
PERUWELZ	27.11.18		Office Dump moved from BELOEIL to PERUWELZ.	
"	28.11.18		A.D.O.S 1st Corps vacated Dump. Authority given for reduction of ten Corps Lorries until 30th	
"	28.11.18		Railhead moved from HARETIN to TOURNAI.	

30-11-18.

W Davick Capt
T.K.A.S.C.
58th Division

War Diary
of
DADOS 56th Division
for
December 1918

[signature] Major
DADOS
56th Division

Army Form C. 2118.

WAR DIARY
or
INTELLIGENCE SUMMARY.

(Erase heading not required.)

Instructions regarding War Diaries and Intelligence Summaries are contained in F. S. Regs., Part II. and the Staff Manual respectively. Title pages will be prepared in manuscript.

Place	Date	Hour	Summary of Events and Information	Remarks and references to Appendices
PERUWELZ	2/12/18		26 D.A.S.A. DC Marched for Demobilisation from 22nd Corps	
"	3/12/18		No. 6 Mob. Workshop, Nos 5, 12 & 35 Motor Lorries Section "A" Aberdeen 55 Am Sec	
"	5/12/18		28, 41, 57, 72 Labour Coys Marched for demobilisation	
"	8/12/18		Conference of Quartermasters at 174 Div H.Qrs.	
"	9/12/18		ADOS 1st Corps visited Dumps	
"	11/12/18		Railhead moved to LEUZE	
"	12/12/18		10,000 Pullovers issued	
"	14/12/18		MAJOR K.C. GREIG DADOS returned from leave	
"	15/12/18		DDOS 1st Army visited Dump. Col PATRICK AOD proceeded to 1st Corps Troops	
"	25/12/18		Railhead moved to LEUZE	
"	31/12/18		3,20 Nearest demands	

Major
DADOS
Corps Troops

J.C. Short
DADOS
1st Corps

Army Form C. 2118.

WAR DIARY
or
INTELLIGENCE SUMMARY.
(Erase heading not required.)

58/J.D./26

War Diary of 58th Div. Train
For
January 1918

Acting Major
D.A.D.T.
58th Div.

WAR DIARY
or
INTELLIGENCE SUMMARY.
(Erase heading not required.)

Army Form C. 2118.

Instructions regarding War Diaries and Intelligence Summaries are contained in F. S. Regs., Part II. and the Staff Manual respectively. Title pages will be prepared in manuscript.

Place	Date	Hour	Summary of Events and Information	Remarks and references to Appendices
PERUWELZ	1/1/19		Hqrs & Bn.H.Q. at PERUWAIZ. Rankine Tournai	
	10/1/19		Rankine moved to LEUZE	
	10/1/19		Major K.C. GREIG DADOS. (on leave from 18/1/19 to 25/1/19)	
	20/1/19		Major MURPHY A/ADOS. worked Temps	
				31/1/19

K Greig Major
A/DADOS
5th Div

Army Form C. 2118.

WAR DIARY
or
INTELLIGENCE SUMMARY.
(Erase heading not required.)

War Diary of "D" 52nd Battery R.F.A.
for February 1919

Kitchener Major
OC D/52

WAR DIARY
or
INTELLIGENCE SUMMARY.
(Erase heading not required.)

Army Form C. 2118.

Instructions regarding War Diaries and Intelligence Summaries are contained in F.S. Regs., Part II. and the Staff Manual respectively. Title pages will be prepared in manuscript.

Place	Date	Hour	Summary of Events and Information	Remarks and references to Appendices
PERUWELZ	5/1/19		58th Div T (Coy) A.S.C. Transferred to D.A.D.O.S. 24th Div.	
"	20/1/19		271 Coy R.T. Transferred from D.A.D.O.S. 7th Div.	
"	23/1/19		Meeting A.D.O.S. 1st Corps. Conference	
"	26/1/19		A.D.O.S. 1st Corps under Divns.	
"	27/1/19		99th Labour Coy. Transferred to D.A.D.O.S. 24th Div.	
"	28/1/19		6th Bn. London Rgt. Transferred to D.A.D.O.S. 3rd Div.	
			2nd Div.	
			9th Div.	
	29/1/19			

Kitching Major
D.A.D.O.S
58th Divn.

Army Form C. 2118.

D.A.D.O.S.
58TH
(LONDON DIVISION)

No. ....

WAR DIARY
or
INTELLIGENCE SUMMARY.
(Erase heading not required.)

Instructions regarding War Diaries and Intelligence Summaries are contained in F. S. Regs., Part II. and the Staff Manual respectively. Title pages will be prepared in manuscript.

Vol 27

Place	Date	Hour	Summary of Events and Information	Remarks and references to Appendices
			War Diary D.A.D.O.S. 58th Div. for March 1919	
	1/4/19		Acting Major D.A.D.O.S. 58th Div.	

T2134. Wt. W708—776. 500000. 4/15. Sir J. C. & S.

Army Form C. 2118.

WAR DIARY
or
INTELLIGENCE SUMMARY.
(Erase heading not required.)

Instructions regarding War Diaries and Intelligence Summaries are contained in F.S. Regs., Part II. and the Staff Manual respectively. Title pages will be prepared in manuscript.

Place	Date	Hour	Summary of Events and Information	Remarks and references to Appendices
PERUWELZ	3/3/19		A Coy Buffs Regt moved to 34th Div.	
"	11/3/19		2 Learners out for Demobilization	
"	17/3/19		137 O.Rs from Coy moved to X.J.H. Dum (Return of 26th Div A.S.C. Mech. Trans. Motor Ambce Show.)	
TOURNAI	27/3/19		Office & Dump moved to TOURNAI. Finished moving from PERUWELZ to TOURNAI	
"	28/3/19		26th D. L/g.a. Base Meal. Tptr. Motor Ambce. Shipped	
"	31/3/19		59th Div. M.T. Coy moved from 24th Divn to 59th Divn.	
	1/4/19			

Signed
Major
D.A.D.T.

Army Form C. 2118.

WAR DIARY
or
INTELLIGENCE SUMMARY.
(Erase heading not required.)

Vol 28

War Diary of D.D.O.S.
53rd Division
from
April 1919

Army Form C. 2118.

WAR DIARY
or
INTELLIGENCE SUMMARY.
(Erase heading not required.)

Instructions regarding War Diaries and Intelligence Summaries are contained in F. S. Regs., Part II. and the Staff Manual respectively. Title pages will be prepared in manuscript.

Place	Date	Hour	Summary of Events and Information	Remarks and references to Appendices
TOURNAI	8/4/19		Lieuten. J.C.S. NAREW ret. from 24th Divn	
	10/4/19		Major F.D.O.S. Vancouver	
	11/4/19		A.D.O.S. visited Office + I.C.S.	
	12/4/19		D.D.O.S. visited Office + I.C.S.	
			Major K.C. GREIG proceeded on leave	
	14/4/19		Lorry sent to CAMPS with advance stores.	
	15/4/19		Col. PARR visited A.D.O.S. MONS.	
	16/4/19		D.D.O.S. visited I.C.S Lieut CROTHERS reported from 6th Divn	
	18/4/19		for duty at I.C.S.	
	23/4/19		A.D.O.S. visited I.C.S.	
	29/4/19		Major K.C. GREIG returned from leave	

116/9.9

Army Form C. 2118.

WAR DIARY
or
INTELLIGENCE SUMMARY.
(Erase heading not required.)

War Diary of 2nd Bn
58th on Form
for May 1917

H.Spencer Major
F.A.D.C.
58th Bn

Record Sek.

Army Form C. 2118.

WAR DIARY
or
INTELLIGENCE SUMMARY.
(Erase heading not required.)

Instructions regarding War Diaries and Intelligence
Summaries are contained in F. S. Regs., Part II.
and the Staff Manual respectively. Title pages
will be prepared in manuscript.

Place	Date	Hour	Summary of Events and Information	Remarks and references to Appendices
TOURNAI	1/5/19 to 31/5/19		Office & Dump & O.C. & H. Ormeau Refreshment Room. Mongoose M. MEZZ. Personnel much by ADOS thinner nothing to report	
	31/5/19		Harvey Major D.D.M.S. 58th Div	

www.ingramcontent.com/pod-product-compliance
Lightning Source LLC
Chambersburg PA
CBHW081453160426
43193CB00013B/2467